The Elizabethan Image of Africa

Eldred D. Jones

D1637148

Published for
The Folger Shakespeare Library
by
The University Press of Virginia

The University Press of Virginia

First published 1971

Title-page illustration: Figure representing Africa
from the frontispiece of
Abraham Ortelius's *Theatrum orbis terrarum* (Antwerp, 1595).

Standard Book Number: 8139–0335–1
Library of Congress Catalog Card Number: 76–160290
Printed in the United States of America

Illustrations

Folger Booklets on Tudor and Stuart Civilization is a series designed to describe various aspects of the cultural history of the sixteenth and seventeenth centuries. Other booklets in the series of related interest to the present one are *Dutch Influences on English Culture, 1558–1625,* by D. W. Davies, and *The Elizabethan Image of Italy,* by John L. Lievsay. For further information, write: The Folger Shakespeare Library, Washington, D.C. 20003.

Sources

BY THE END of the sixteenth century, the inquiring Englishman had access to a quite impressive body of authentic information on Africa in the form of published accounts of actual sea voyages and land travels and fairly accurate maps, particularly of the coastal areas. This information did not, however, wholly displace the legendary ideas and fancies that had taken root in the popular imagination before these more authentic accounts became available. The result was a rich mixture of fact, myth, and fancy.

Before the middle of the sixteenth century, Englishmen derived their ideas of Africa from the Bible, the classical historians, and contemporary books that retailed such knowledge. These ancient sources continued to be cited long after English mariners not only had visited Africa but had published accounts of their voyages that described personal encounters with the peoples of the coastal areas with whom they had traded. They had met African kings, had made friends with ordinary people, had dined on oysters, and had brought back pepper, gold dust, and elephants' teeth from West Africa. However even these accounts sometimes helped to confuse the true picture since they appeared on the same pages as the legendary accounts of the monsters and strange beings that peopled the pages of the classical historians. Within the same covers the shadowy figure of Prester John jostles for space with the flesh and blood of the king of Benin.

Thus for a time, even if he wanted to, the sixteenth-century reader might well have found it difficult to separate the true from the imaginary. On a few occasions, indeed, ancient and modern sources truthfully corroborated one another. Thus Ben Jonson could cite both the ancient authorities and the near-contemporary Joannes Leo Africanus in support of the ideas underlying his *Masque of Blackness*. He wrote: "Pliny, Solinus, Ptolomey, and of late Leo the African, remember unto us a river in Aethiopia, famous by the name of Niger; of which the people were called *Nigritae,* now Negroes, and are the blackest nation of the world." Jonson then went on to make his characters "daughters of Niger" and on this good authority represented them on the stage as Negroes.

Leo's book, which Jonson cited, was translated into English as *A Geographical History of Africa,* but it had been published in Italy in 1550 and was known to Englishmen even before John Pory's English translation of 1600. A French edition of this, the most authentic account of the interior of Africa, is listed among the contents of the library of Sir Thomas Smith (1513–77), one of the most prominent statesmen and scholars of the day. Richard Willes mentioned the work in his dedicatory epistle to *The History of Travel* (1577), and George Puttenham in *The Art of English Poesie* (1589) cited the work of "Iahan Leon" before an English translation was available. Richard Eden, who had used Giovanni Battista Ramusio's work, in which Leo's material was first published in 1550, must also have known the work in the original. Robert Greene, in his *Farewell to Folly,* referred to the love of Abusahid, king of Fez, for the wife of Cosimo de Cheri, "as Leon in his description of Affrike setteth down." This reference also preceded the English translation.

After Pory's translation references became even more numerous. There is strong circumstantial evidence indicating that Shakespeare also knew the book and that its background material is reflected in *Othello* and *Antony and Cleopatra.* Leo's colorful biography alone, which Pory prefixed to his translation, would have attracted enough attention to the book. Leo, a North African Moor, had traveled widely in Africa before he was captured in the Mediterranean and presented to Pope Leo X, who converted him to Christianity and gave him his name at baptism. The similarity between Leo's biography and that of Othello is striking.

Ancient History

The foundations of knowledge about Africa had, however, been firmly laid by the classical historians before Leo wrote his ac-

count. Both Herodotus and Pliny had distinguished Egypt from
the rest of Africa. Herodotus, in B. R.'s Elizabethan translation of
1584, had made the distinction clear: "The Grecian writers are in

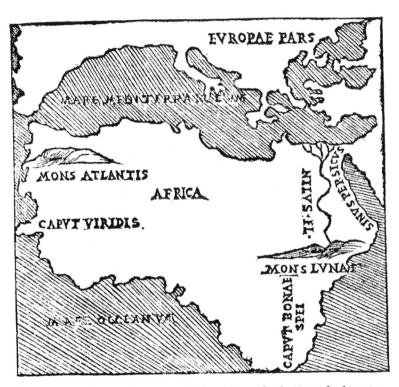

Illus. 1. An early woodcut map of Africa from Pliny's *Naturalis historiae*
(Venice, 1525). A comparison with Abraham Ortelius's map (Illus. 14, p.
38) illustrates the advances in geographical knowledge made during the age
of discovery.

a wrong box, . . . making but three parts of the whole earth,
Europa, Asia, and Africa: whereas of necessity Delta in Aegypt
should be accounted for the fourth, since by their own books it is
neither joined with Asia, nor yet with Africa" (sigs. Lır-Lıv).
Pliny too wrote "the inhabited country next to Africa is Egypt."

3

These historians wrote in great detail about the laws, manners, and customs of Egypt, but of "Africa" they were less knowledgeable; so they relied on stories and legends. The strangeness, mystery, and wildness which characterized Africa in men's minds must have sprung from tales like Herodotus's account of the five intrepid young gentlemen who ventured from the beaten track and went into "Africa":

Five of them being assigned thereto by lot, put themselves in voyage to go search and descry the wilderness and desert places of Africa, to the end they might see more and make further report thereof than ever any that had attempted the same. For the seacoast of Africa pointing to the North Pole, many nations do inhabit, beginning from Aegypt, and continuing to the promontory named Soloes, wherein Africa hath his end and bound. All the places above the sea are haunted with wild and savage beasts, being altogether void and desolate, pestered with sand, and exceeding dry. These gentlemen-travelers having made sufficient provision of water and other viands necessary for their journey, first of all passed the countries that were inhabited: and next after that, came into the wild and waste regions amongst the caves and dens of fierce and untamed beasts, through which they held on their way to the west part of the earth. In which manner, after they had continued many days' journey and traveled over a great part of the sandy countries, they came at length to espy certain fair and goodly trees growing in a fresh and pleasant meadow; whereunto incontinently making repair and tasting the fruit that grew thereon, they were suddenly surprised and taken short by a company of little dwarfs, far under the common pitch and stature of men, whose tongue the gentlemen knew not, neither was their speech understood of them. Being apprehended, they were led away over sundry pools and meres into a city, where all the inhabitants were of the same stature and degree with those that had taken them, and of color swart and black. Fast by the side of this city ran a swift and violent river, flowing from the west to the east, wherein were to be seen very hideous and terrible serpents called crocodiles. To this end drew the talk of Etearchus, king of the Ammonians, save that he added besides how the Namasonian [Nasamonian] gentlemen returned home to their own country . . . and how the people also of the city whither they were brought were all conjurers, and given to the study of the black art. The flood that had his passage by the city, Etearchus supposed to be the river Nilus, even as also reason itself giveth it to be [sigs. L5v–L6r].

Herodotus's account, though it relates a story that may have had some authenticity, describes an adventure into the interior of Africa that took place before his time—he died about 424 B.C. This translation of his work gave Elizabethan readers, even if they could not read Greek, what must have seemed to them an authentic source for some of their notions about Africa. It was by no means the first of such works, but it was an actual translation from "the Father of History" himself rather than a secondhand account, of which there were quite a few.

Pliny, whose Latin was more accessible to the Elizabethans than Herodotus's Greek, gave descriptions of the interior of Africa which were retailed by popular writers and also made possible the imagery of the Elizabethan poets and playwrights by providing their readers and audiences with the necessary background to understand what otherwise would have been inexplicable images. For those who could not read Latin there were also convenient summaries and translations.

Popular Digests

In 1556 there appeared *A Summary of the Antiquities and Wonders of the World . . . Out of the Sixteen First Books of . . . Pliny.* It was meant to be a popular work, and was. (More scholarly translations were also available such as Philemon Holland's Pliny of 1601.) The *Summary* retails some of the extraordinary types who, according to Pliny, peopled the interior of Africa. Here is a sample:

Of the Ethiopians there are divers forms and kinds of men. Some there are toward the east that have neither nose nor nostrils, but the face all full. Others that have no upper lip, they are without tongues, and they speak by signs, and they have but a little hole to take their breath at, by the which they drink with an oaten straw. There are some called Syrbote that are eight foot high, they live with the chase of elephants. In a part of Affricke be people called Ptoemphane, for their king they have a dog, at whose fancy they are governed . . . . Toward the west there is a people called Arimaspi, that hath but one eye in their foreheads, they are in the desert and wild country. The people called Agriphagi live with the flesh of panthers and lions: and the people called Anthropomphagi which we call cannibals, live with human flesh. The Cinamolgi, their heads are almost like to the heads of dogs. . . . In Libie which is at the end of the Ethiopes, there are people differing from the common order of others, they have among them no names and they curse the sun for his great heat, by the which they are all black saving their teeth and a little the palm of their hands, and they never dream. . . . Others called Gramantes, they make no marriages, but all women are common. Gamphasantes they go all naked. Blemmyis a people so called, they have no heads, but have their mouth and their eyes in their breasts. And others there are that go [walk] more by training of their hands than with their feet [sigs. B3v–B4v].*

What a feast of wonders! Shakespeare never forgot them; neither did the more learned Ben Jonson who, as was his habit, probably went to the original sources and not to popular summaries.

In spite of the fact that information on Africa had been available earlier directly from the classics and even from popular English summaries of them, 1555 is a convenient date from which to start a review of the Elizabethan image of Africa, for in that year two books appeared that typify the two sources of popular notions of Africa. William Waterman's *The Fardle of Fashions* owed its allegiance, through Johan Boemus, to "the father of stories Herodotus the Greek" and other ancient authorities including Pliny. Richard Eden on the other hand, in his translation of Peter Martyr's *Decades of the New World,* included the first two published accounts of actual voyages made by Englishmen to Africa in the sixteenth century. It is true that even in Peter

---

* Throughout the booklet, spelling is modernized in quotations with the exception of names of places and tribes. Modern spelling, if it can be found, is given in brackets or at the bottom of the page unless the names are clearly identifiable. *Syrbote:* Syrbotae; *Ptoemphane:* Ptoemphani; *Agriphagi:* Agriophagi; *Anthropomphagi:* Anthropophagi; *Cinamolgi:* Cynamolgi; *Libie:* Libya; *Gramantes:* Garamantes; *Blemmyis:* Blemmyes.

Martyr's pages the reports of eyewitnesses stood side by side with some of the ancient material, but the process by which new information replaced the old had begun. The transformation was slow; indeed one might say it still goes on. Legends die hard in the popular mind, while facts tend to languish in books.

Waterman's *Fardle* (1555) was a translation of Boemus's *Omnium gentium mores* (1520), which had formed the basis of William Prat's earlier *Description of the Country of Africa* (1554). Waterman's book presented afresh for English readers the old legends supplemented by the more recent though often no less fanciful material of Sir John Mandeville. Boemus treated Egypt as a part of Africa, as by the sixteenth century it had come to be regarded, but in deference to his ancient authorities he qualified his classification. Waterman's translation reads: "Aegipte is a country lying in Affrike, or as some hold opinion, bordering thereupon." The translation may have revived old fancies, but it also presented (at least in English) some new material. For many readers the distinction between Prester John and his subjects must have been new information: "And he is not as the most of the Ethiopians are, black, but white." The postprandial activities of the fish-eating Ichthyophagi must have attracted comment:

They eat as I have said in the wild field together abroad, rejoicing with a semblance of merriness and a manner of singing full untuned. That done they fall upon their women, even as they come to hand without any choice: utterly void of care, by reason they are alway sure of meat in good plenty [sigs. G1v–G2r].

Passages such as this would have cemented in the popular mind notions of dark-skinned people as carefree and lustful, notions that were taken for granted by mid-century.

The two opening chapters of the *Fardle* give, respectively, "the true opinion of the divine concerning the beginning of man" and "the false opinion of the philosopher concerning the beginning of man." The second, oddly enough,

affirmed the Ethopiens to have been the first of all men. For they conjectured that the ground of that country lying nearest the heats

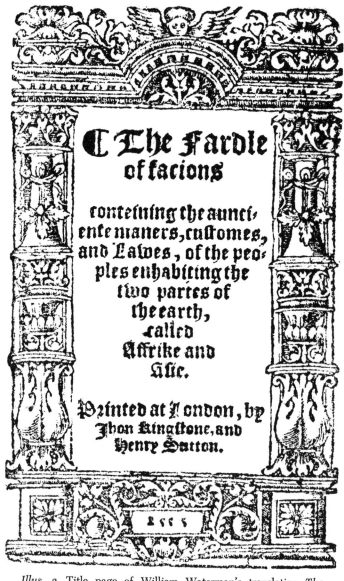

Illus. 2. Title page of William Waterman's translation *The Fardle of Fashions* (London, 1555).

of the sun must needs first of all other wax warm. And the earth at that time being but clammy and soft, through the attemperance of that moisture and heat, man there first to have been formed, and there to have gladlier inhabited (as native and natural unto him) than in any other place, when all places were as yet strange, and unknown, which after men sought [sigs. B6v–B7r].

(This notion does not sound so strange today after the discoveries of Dr. Louis S. Leakey in the Olduvai Gorge that locate the earliest known human fossils in Africa.) Although Boemus implicitly rejected the theory that life started in Africa, he nevertheless began his description of the "three parts" of the earth with Africa.

The Ethiopians ("Ethiopes") took their name, according to the book, either from "Ethiopus, Vulcan's son," or else from "the Greek words *aythoo* and *ops,* whereof the former signifieth to broil, or to burn up with heat, and the other in the eye or sight. Which showeth in effect, that the country lying in the eye of the sun, it must needs be of heat almost importable." The heat of Africa became a frequent source of imagery.

The king of the Ethiopians was of course Prester John, "a man of such power, that he is reported to have under him threescore and two other kings." Gold was plentiful and hence little regarded, so that when the ambassadors of Cambyses visited the Macrobii on the island of Meroë, they "found the prisoners in the jail fettered and tied with chains of gold"! Egypt is described: its annual inundation, its laws, its customs, and its religion.

Finally comes the most sensational section on the interior of Africa, that describing the strange peoples. However not all the peoples described are monsters as in, for example, *A Summary of Antiquities* cited earlier. Indeed, some of the descriptions were employed as vehicles of mild satire against Europe. The Troglodytes, for example, "have their head over them, whom they call Tiraunt [tyrant]. But not meaning in him so much tyranny in deed, as some time some of our governors under a fairer name do execute." Such approving glosses, however, pale before the parade of Acridophagi, Ichthyophagi, Ilophagi, Spermatophagi, and a whole list of others.

III.

EFFIGIATIO Æthiopum, qui funt in Moſſambica, Caffres nominatorum.

Affres *Æthiopes funt ad oram maritimam, qua ad caput vſq̃, bonæ ſpei porrigitur, colore nigerrimi, capillis criſpis, naribus ſimis, labiis tumentibus, labiis geniſq̃, perforatis, appendẽtibus vel oſsibus, vel margaritis; corpus faciemq̃, vt plurimum inurunt ferro candente ad formã telæ Damaſcenæ ſericæ, nudi prorſus currunt. eorũ tamen vxores, qui in Moſſambica habitant, pudenda obuelant propter Luſitanorum conuerſationem, à quibus telam bombycinam in permutatione auri & eboris accipiunt. Integuntur autem à mammillis ad media vſq̃, femora, idq̃, feminæ, at viri vix nuda pudẽda breui panniculo abdunt. Alij in Moſſambica funt Mahumetani, alij Pythagorici, alij Chriſtiani, reliqui ad vſq̃, caput bonæ ſpei nullam omnino DEI notitiam habent, viuunt brutorum more. qua de re vide plura cap. 4 & 41.*

DE CAF.

Illus. 3. Illustration from Johann Theodor de Bry's *India Orientalis*, Pt. 2 (Frankfurt, 1599), a part of Jan Huygen van Linschoten's *Itinerario*, depicting the inhabitants of Mozambique. The text gives a description of their appearance, customs, and religions.

Eyewitnesses

As has been indicated, 1555 saw the publication of the first two accounts of English voyages to Africa. English seamen had been discouraged from making voyages down the West Coast of Africa by two papal bulls that gave the monopoly of penetration in these areas to the Portuguese. While England remained Catholic, these bulls were generally respected, and as late as 1555 the Portuguese ambassador in London was able to press for the enforcement of the ban. Although this did not stop English voyages altogether, it delayed the establishment of regular English trade. (By comparison the Portuguese began the building of their fort Elmina in Ghana [modern] in 1481.) However, there were some voyages on the part of Englishmen despite the ban, and Richard Eden published, along with his translation of Peter Martyr's *Decades of the New World,* the accounts of Thomas Windham's voyage to Guinea in 1553 and John Lok's voyage to Mina (Elmina) in 1554–55. These accounts are most interesting for they show how great a hold popular lore can have on the mind, even in the face of more factual information.

Prefixed to the actual account of the first voyage, is "A brief description of Affrike" gathered by Eden. This includes some reasonably factual information but also an uncritical repetition of old beliefs. In an account which goes on to give a very interesting description of the court of Benin we also have references to Prester John, the legendary king. In the same volume that describes eyewitness accounts of the elaborate courtesy of some of the inhabitants of the Guinea Coast, we read in this "gathered" preface: "But all the regions of Guinea are pure gentiles and idolaters without profession of any religion, or other knowledge of God, than by the law of nature." It is difficult to see how Eden reconciled that passage with the following account of the visit to Benin.

When they came they were brought with a great company to the presence of the king [of Benin], who being a black Moor (although not so black as the rest) sat in a great huge hall, long and wide, the walls made of earth without windows, the roof of thin boards, open in sundry places, like unto louvers to let in the air.

And here to speak of the great reverence they give to their king, being such that if we would give as much to our Saviour Christ, we should remove from our heads many plagues which we daily deserve for our contempt and impiety. . . .

And now to speak somewhat of the communication that was between the king and our men, you shall first understand that he himself could speak the Portugal tongue, which he had learned of a child. Therefore after that he had commanded our men to stand up and demanded of them the cause of their coming into that country, they answered by Pinteado that they were merchants traveling into those parts for the commodities of his country for exchange of wares which they had brought from their countries, being such as should be no less commodious for him and his people [sigs. 4S2v–4S3r].

Somehow this account of an actual meeting with a civilized, bilingual, black king in Guinea (he had even offered the strangers credit until their next voyage) did not impress Eden enough to make him modify the sweeping generalizations he had "gathered" for his preface.

The second account, that of John Lok's voyage, contains even more extreme "gatherings" from the early historians, and this time not even as a preface but mixed in with the actual facts. Thus almost straight out of Pliny comes a passage like this one:

It is to understand, that the people which now inhabit the regions of the coast of Guinea and the middle parts of Affrica, as Lybia the inner and Nubia, with divers other great and large regions about the same, were in old time called Ethiopes and Nigrite, which we now call Moors, Moorens, or Negroes, a people of beastly living, without a God, law, religion, or commonwealth, and so scorched and vexed with the heat of the sun that in many places they curse it when it riseth [sig. 4V3v].

Trooping out of the pages of Pliny also come the Ichthyophagi, the Rhapsii, and the Anthropophagi. Yet in the same account, we have descriptions of contacts with actual people whose languages were recorded, whose houses, manners, and crafts were described, and from whom in addition the merchants made large profits.

 ARIÆ animalium in hoc regno inueniuntur species, vt supra cap. 10. primi libri videre est. Sed cum quædam etiam in hisce nostris inueniantur regionibus, peregrina & alias ignota hisce iconibus exprimere conati sumus, vt lectorem eorum formis in cerebro effigiandis leuemus tædio. Primum itaque est quod Dante appellant incolæ, corporis forma (statura enim minus paulo est) bouem referens, nisi quod cornua longa, caprinis cornubus similia, & perpolita habeat in capite. Venatori adeo infestum, vt nisi celerrimus sit & dexterrimus, facile eum conculcet. Secundum est Empalanga, boui quoque per omnia simile, nisi quod pectore & capite, cerui in morem, incedat erecto, & cornua gerat oblonga ab inferiori parte nodosa & interius inflexa. Mentionem quoque eodem capite fecimus animalis cuiusdam draconem referentis, ab incolis olim studiose nutriti & pro Deo habiti, cuius quoque effigiem delineauimus, vna cum lupo furtum suum dorso ferente, & simiis magnatum deliciis: & demum serpente bullam in cauda gerente medicinalem: quorum omnium descriptionem suo loco proposuimus.

Illus. 4. The elephants and monkeys combined with the dragon and the serpent with a medicine ball in its tail illustrate the mixture of fact and fancy in books available to Elizabethan readers. From de Bry's *India Orientalis*, Pt. 1 (Frankfurt, 1598), an edition of Filippo Pigafetta's version of Duarte Lopes's *Congo*.

Thus fact and fancy were indissolubly mixed in the same accounts and, consequently, in the popular mind.

For the common reader as well as for the imaginative writer, all this was pure gold. For the merchants it was literally that. The information on trade commodities—gold, pepper, and ivory—aroused the interests of merchants and opened the way for subsequent voyages. Though intending venturers might well have been daunted by accounts of the "smothering heat with close and cloudy air and storming weather of such putrifying quality that it rotted the coats off their backs," they would have been encouraged by accounts of the sophisticated king of Benin and the prospect of receiving credit from him. What they thought about the prospect of meeting men without heads we cannot tell, but it did not deter them from venturing forth. Descriptions of those strange creatures together with factual information on the real inhabitants blended to fertilize the imagination of poets and playwrights, and it was from such conflicting material that the background and even suggestions for the language of *Othello* derived.

Not only did Elizabethans read about Africans from published accounts, they must also have heard even taller stories in private homes and public houses from returning sailors who often brought back strange trophies from their intrepid voyages to give verisimilitude to their otherwise improbable narratives.

When Lok returned from Mina in 1555, he brought back "four hundred pound weight and odd of gold, of twenty-two carats and one grain in fineness; also thirty-six butts of grains [pepper] and about two hundred and fifty elephants' teeth of all quantities." This was sensational enough, but the *pièce de résistance* of that voyage was an elephant's head which seems to have been put on exhibition in the house of a London merchant named Sir Andrew Judde. Richard Eden saw the exhibit himself, and wrote:

At this last voyage, was brought from Guinea the head of an elephant of such huge bigness that only the bones or cranew [skull] thereof, beside the nether jaw and great tusks, weighed about two hundred weight and was as much as I could well lift from the ground. . . . This head divers have seen in the house of the worthy merchant, Sir Andrew Judde, where also I saw it and beheld it not only with my

Illus. 5. Picture of an elephant from Edward Topsell's *The History of Four-Footed Beasts* (London, 1607).

bodily eyes, but much more with the eyes of my mind and spirit considered by the work the cunning and wisdom of the workmaster: without which consideration the sight of such strange and wonderful things may rather seem curiosities than profitable contemplations [sig. 4V2r].

There follows a detailed description of elephants: their appearance, habits, and their continual war with dragons who "desire their blood because it is very cold"!

Negroes in England

Even more of an attraction for the curious would have been the Africans who from the earliest English voyages were brought back to England. After the 1554 voyage to Guinea, Lok's men

15

"brought with them certain black slaves, whereof some were tall and strong men and could well agree with our meats and drinks." Two of these men returned with William Towerson on a subsequent voyage in 1556 and acted as interpreters and public relations men for him in West Africa. When on one occasion the inhabitants in one area refused to treat with Towerson, he used one of his Negroes to smooth the way for him:

We found a fair bay where we ran in and found a small town . . . , but the Negroes in a long time would not come to us, but at the last by the persuasion of our own Negroes, one boat came to us, and with him we sent George our Negro ashore, and after he had talked with them, they came aboard our boats without fear [Richard Hakluyt, *Principal Navigations* (1598–1600), II, 3D1v].

This same account mentions two other Negroes, "Anthonie and Binne," who had remained in London, and who, according to Towerson, were due to return to West Africa on a subsequent voyage.

Eden's accounts were republished along with other voyages in Richard Hakluyt's historic *Principal Navigations*. This work, first published in one volume in 1589 and issued in final form in three volumes (1598–1600), is a comprehensive collection of accounts of English voyages all round the world. Hakluyt intended his work to remove the stigma of lack of enterprise from English sailors whose achievements suffered in comparison with those of their Continental counterparts. The work achieved much more. It boosted morale in general, fired the imagination of writers, and, as Louis B. Wright has suggested (in *Middle-Class Culture in Elizabethan England*, p. 548), left lasting marks on English prose.

The free movement of Negroes, apparently with their consent, between West Africa and England was soon shattered by the triangular slaving voyages, such as Sir John Hawkins's three voyages of 1562, 1564, and 1567. More and more Africans (now certainly deprived of their freedom) continued to be brought to England, and thus there was plenty of opportunity for Englishmen in London and other ports to see Africans of various shades of color from the middle of the sixteenth century onward. Not

Illus. 6. The crest of Sir John Hawkins, the first regular English slave trader. The crest incorporates captive Africans. From M. W. S. Hawkins, *Plymouth Armada Heroes* (Plymouth, 1888). Library of Congress copy.

only is it certain that Shakespeare, living as he did in London and being so much a part of his times, would have had the opportunity to see Negroes, it seems impossible that he could have escaped seeing them. Until very recently the presence in fair numbers of black West Africans in England in the sixteenth and seventeenth centuries was ignored by critics of Elizabethan and Jacobean

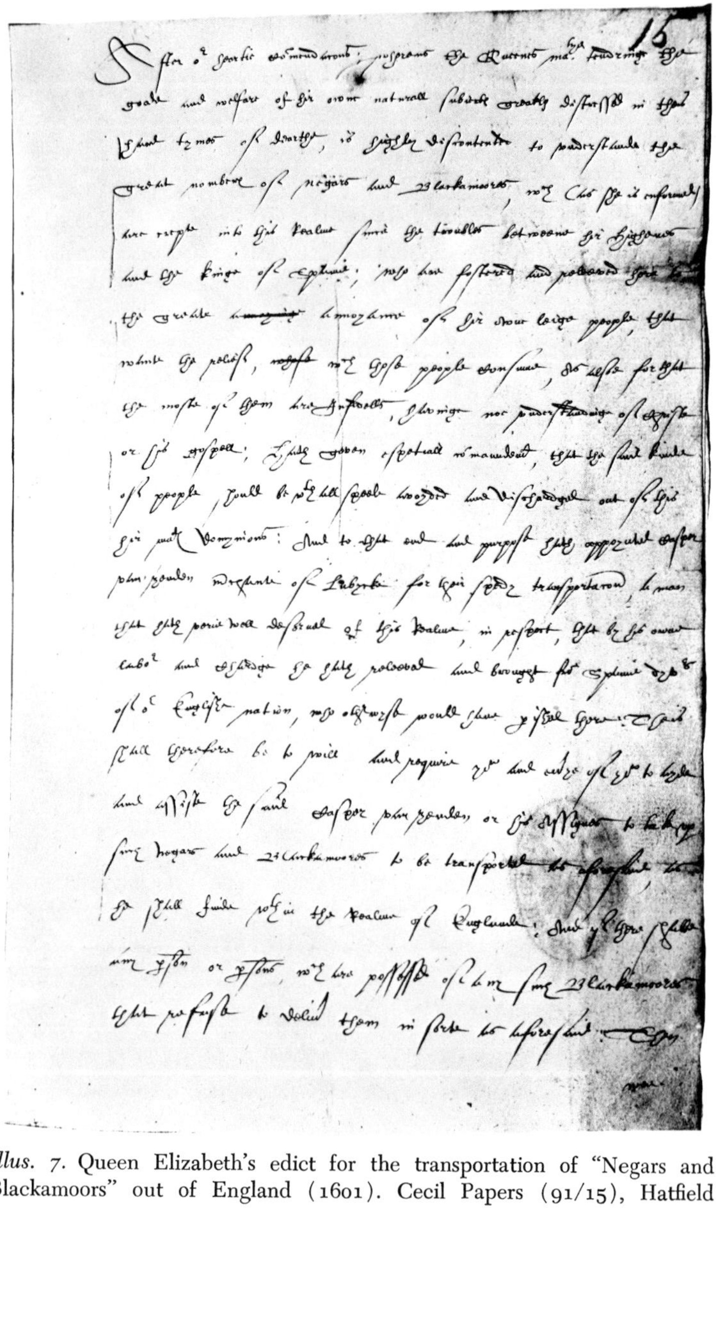

Illus. 7. Queen Elizabeth's edict for the transportation of "Negars and Blackamoors" out of England (1601). Cecil Papers (91/15), Hatfield

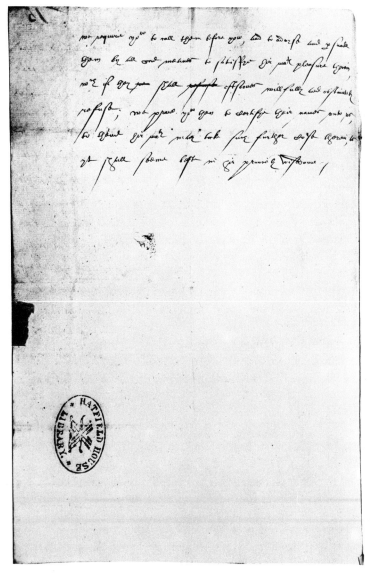

House, Hatfield, England. Reproduced by permission of the Marquess of Salisbury.

drama, who consequently have made quite erroneous statements about Shakespeare's conception of Othello.

Contact with North Africa had been even earlier than with West Africa, and travelers to the Continent, particularly Spain, would have seen light-skinned Moors. We have a definite reference in an account of Windham's 1551 voyage to North Africa of North African Moors being returned to their country from England. "There were two Moors being noblemen, whereof one was of the king's blood, conveyed by the said Master Thomas Windham into their country out of England" (*Principal Navigations*, II, 3A4v).

The Negro population in England grew steadily from the middle of the century. W. E. Miller cites two assessments of strangers in the parish of All Hallows, London, in 1599 that give the names of four Negroes, three of whom were female, living in the parish (*Notes and Queries*, [CCVI], New Ser., VIII [1961], 138). By the end of the century, in fact, Queen Elizabeth had begun to be "discontented" at the "great numbers of Negars and Blackamoors which . . . are crept into this realm," and issued two edicts, one in 1599 and a stronger one in 1601, in which she complained of the influx and appointed a certain Caspar van Zenden (Zeuden), a merchant of Lübeck, to transport them out of the country. The later decree reads:

After our hearty commendations; whereas the Queen's Majesty, tendering the good and welfare of her own natural subjects greatly distressed in these hard times of dearth, is highly discontented to understand the great numbers of Negars and Blackamoors which (as she is informed) are crept into this realm since the troubles between Her Highness and the King of Spain, who are fostered and relieved here to the great annoyance of her own liege people that want the relief which those people consume; as also for that the most of them are infidels, having no understanding of Christ or his Gospel, hath given especial commandment that the said kind of people should be with all speed avoided and discharged out of this Her Majesty's dominions. And to that end and purpose hath appointed Caspar van Zenden, merchant of Lübeck for their speedy transportation, a man that hath very well deserved of this realm in respect that by his own labor and charge he hath relieved and brought from Spain divers of our English nation who otherwise would have perished there. This shall therefore be to will and require you and every of you to aid and assist the said Caspar van Zenden or his assigns to take up such Negars and Blackamoors to be transported as aforesaid, as he shall find within the realm of England. And if there shall be any person or persons which are possessed of any such Blackamoors that refuse to deliver them in sort as aforesaid, then we require you to call them before you and to advise and persuade them by all good means to satisfy Her Majesty's pleasure therein, which if they shall eftsoons willfully and obstinately refuse, we pray you then to certify their names unto us, to the end Her Majesty may take such further course therein as it shall seem best in her princely wisdom [Cecil Papers, 91/15].

Pory and Leo

Leo's *Geographical History of Africa* has been mentioned earlier as a very influential work on the interior of Africa. The interior was the area about which factual information had been most lacking, and it was this void that Leo's book filled with people rather than with the earlier monsters. Leo, like all good travel writers, had his own firm opinions and even prejudices which livened up the descriptions, particularly of nations he disapproved of.

Pory prefaced his translation of the work with "A Description of places undescribed by John Leo." This shows clearly that in a mind like Pory's the recent accounts had begun to displace the hallowed legends. There is still ignorance, prejudice, and disapproval in some of Pory's accounts, but his picture of the coast of Guinea shows the more enlightened state of knowledge that was the result of works like Abraham Hartwell's translation (1597) of Filippo Pigafetta's edition of Duarte Lopes's *Congo* (1591), and William Phillip's translation (1598) of Jan Huygen van Linschoten's *Voyages* (1596). He occasionally resorted to classical names, such as the Ichthyophagi and the Autolatae, but only as peoples inhabiting an area and so called by "the ancient writers." A nice mixture of attitudes is seen in the passage on

A GEOGRAPHICAL
HISTORIE of AFRICA,
Written in Arabicke and Ĵtalian
by IOHN LEO a More, borne
in Granada, and brought vp
in Barbarie.

*Wherein he hath at large deſcribed, not onely the qualities, ſituations, and true
diſtances of the regions, cities, townes, mountaines, riuers, and other places
throughout all the north and principall partes of Africa; but alſo the
deſcents and families of their kings, the cauſes and euents of their warres,
with their manners, cuſtomes, religions, and ciuile gouernment, and
many other memorable matters : gathered partly out of his owne di-
ligent obſeruations, and partly out of the ancient records and Chronicles
of the Arabians and Mores.*

Before which, out of the beſt ancient and moderne writers, is prefixed a generall
deſcription of Africa, and alſo a particular treatiſe of all the maine lands
and Iſles vndeſcribed by *Iohn Leo.*

*And after the ſame is annexed a relation of the great Princes, and the manifold religions
in that part of the world.*

Tranſlated and collected by IOHN PORY, lately
of Goneuill and Caius College
in Cambridge.

LONDINI,
Ĵmpenſis Georg. Biſhop.
1600

Illus. 8. Title page of John Pory's translation of Leo Africanus's *Geographical History of Africa* (London, 1600).

ARGVMENTVM V.

Armatura tam nobiliorum quam gregariorum militum defcripta lib, 1. cap. 7.

Ic quæ de ornatu militari diximus ob oculos ponuntur.
Quomodo nimirum caput variis auium ornent pennis vt
& maiores & terribiliores videantur hoftibus: Superiori
parte corporis nudi, ferreis catenis fe onerant, cingulo quoque tintinabulis quibufdam repleto animum & fibi & fuis
augent. Et quomodo inftrumentum illud pyramidis forma ex tribus
ferri laminis compaſtum pulfantes fonum edant horrendum: &
demum quomodo altero vtantur inftrumento bellico,
ex corio cauæ arboris cortici fuperindito
conftante.

Bb 2   ARGV-

Illus. 9. Illustration from de Bry's edition of the *Congo* depicting a nobleman warrior, his arms, and his attendants.

Benin, an English account of which had already been published by Eden:

Westward from the countries last mentioned lieth the kingdom of Benin, having a very proper town of that name, and an haven called Gurte. The inhabitants live in idolatry, and are a rude and brutish nation; notwithstanding that their prince is served with such high reverence, and never cometh in sight but with great solemnity and many ceremonies; at whose death his chief favorites count it the greatest point of honor to be buried with him, to the end (as they vainly imagine) they may do him service in another world [sig. d3v].

According to Pory, the locusts of Guinea seem to have been as much of a plague as those of Egypt, but they were also potential food—as they had been to John the Baptist in the desert. The description of Sierra Leone is recognizable today even if the height of the mountain now seems exaggerated:

This cape last mentioned [Sierra Leone] hath an exceeding high mountain thereupon, which causeth it to be seen a mighty distance off. It seemeth to be the same promontory which Hanno and Ptolemey call the chariot of the gods. It is called by the name of a lion in regard of the dreadful thunders and lightnings which are continually heard from the top thereof: howbeit near unto it are found apes, monkeys, and such other beasts as live in temperate places [sig. d4r].

If Pory's preface is interesting, then Leo's book itself must have been a veritable *fiat lux*. Not everything Leo wrote is indisputable though he was particular in separating what he himself had seen from what he had obtained second hand. The information he gave on the land of the Negroes was startlingly new to those Elizabethans who could read only English and, ironically, would have been equally strange to most modern historians until the recent revival of interest in precolonial African history. Here is Leo's description of an area that for a long time was peopled with monsters in the popular mind:

Moreover, the land of Negroes is divided into many kingdoms: whereof albeit a great part be unknown unto us, and removed far out of our trade; we will notwithstanding make relation of those places where we ourselves have abode and which by long experience are grown very familiar unto us: as likewise of some other places from whence merchants used to travel unto the same cities wherein myself was then resident. I myself saw fifteen kingdoms of the Negroes howbeit there are many more, which although I saw not with mine own eyes yet are they by the Negroes sufficiently known and frequented. Their names therefore (beginning from the west, and so proceeding eastward and southward) are these following: Gualata, Ghinea, Melli, Tombuto, Gago, Guber, Agadez, Cano, Casena, Zegzeg, Zanfara, Guangara, Burno, Gaoga, Nube [sig. A3r].*

Leo has become for modern historians a source for precolonial African history as he was for Ben Jonson. What he did for Shakespeare is not as definite, since that playwright did not provide marginal notes and glosses as did his more learned contemporary, and further since he often so assimilated his material that it is difficult to identify his minor sources. Lois Whitney in an article "Did Shakespeare know *Leo Africanus?*" (*PMLA*, XXXVII [1922], 470–83) suggests that some passages from Leo's *History*, as well as Pory's prefatory account of his life, influenced Shakespeare's portrayal of Othello. One such passage deals with the women of Numidia and the jealousy of their husbands:

Very civil they are, after their manner, both in speech and gestures: sometimes they will accept of a kiss; but whoso tempteth them farther, putteth his own life in hazard. For by reason of jealousy you may see them daily one to be the death and destruction of another, and that in such savage and brutish manner that in this case they will show no compassion at all. And they seem to be more wise in this behalf than divers of our people, for they will by no means match themselves unto an harlot [sig. B5r].

By no means is this the play *Othello,* or even a sketch for Desdemona, but who is to say what straws in the wind added to the blaze of Shakespeare's imagination? The life of Leo himself as briefly outlined by Pory is suggestive of Othello's history:

* *Gualata:* Walata; *Ghinea:* Guinea; *Melli:* Mali; *Tombuto:* Timbuktu; *Gago:* Gao; *Guber:* Gober; *Agadez:* Agadès; *Cano:* Kano; *Casena:* Katsina; *Zegzeg:* Zaria; *Zanfara:* Zamfara; *Guangara:* Wangara; *Burno:* Bornu; *Gaoga:* Kaoka; *Nube:* Nubia.

Who albeit by birth a Moor, and by religion for many years a Mahumetan, yet if you consider his parentage, wit, education, learning, employments, travels, and his conversion to christianity, you shall find him not altogether unfit to undertake such an enterprise, nor unworthy to be regarded [sig. [A]2v].

Pory's description of Leo, "his parentage seemeth not to have been ignoble," is not exactly

> I fetch my life and being
> From men of royal siege
>
> [I, ii, 21–22]

but in a mind like Shakespeare's one could have led to the other.

Leo, as Pory stated in the preface, was a scholar, a traveler, and a soldier:

For . . . did not he, as himself in his third book witnesseth, personally serve king Mahumet of Fez in his wars against Arzilla? . . . Yea, how often in regard of his singular knowledge and judgment in the laws of those countries was he appointed and sometimes constrained at divers strange cities and towns through which he traveled to become a judge and arbiter in matters of greatest moment? [sig. [A]3r]

In all these adventures, Leo encountered many dangers. He was captured, sold to slavery, and rescued. Without proceeding beyond Pory's preface, the Elizabethan reader would have sensed the thrill of Leo's adventures. If his appetite was sufficiently whetted, he could have followed Pory's directions and turned to the relevant part of the main work. In this way, Pory's preface is an excellent guide for the browser. It is difficult to resist the conclusion that Shakespeare, like Jonson, Puttenham, Greene, and others, read (either in the original or in Pory's translation) passages like this one:

I marvel much how ever he should have escaped so many thousands of imminent dangers. . . . For how many desolate cold mountains, and huge, dry, and barren deserts passed he? How often was he in hazard to have been captived or to have had his throat cut by the prowling Arabians and wild Moors? And how hardly many times escaped he the lion's greedy mouth and the devouring jaws of the crocodile? But if you will needs have a brief journal of his travels, you may see in the end of his eight book what he writeth for himself [sig. [A]3r].

This is not necessarily a direct source for anything Shakespeare wrote, but how suggestive it is, blending as it would have done with the ancient stories of the hazards of the interior as a background for Othello's history:

Her father loved me, oft invited me;
Still questioned me the story of my life
From year to year—the battles, sieges, fortunes
That I have passed.
I ran it through, even from my boyish days
To th' very moment that he bade me tell it.
Wherein I spoke of most disastrous chances,
Of moving accidents by flood and field;
Of hairbreadth scapes i' th' imminent deadly breach;
Of being taken by the insolent foe
And sold to slavery; of my redemption thence
And portance in my travel's history;
Wherein of antres vast and deserts idle,
Rough quarries, rocks, and hills whose heads touch heaven,
It was my hint to speak—such was the process;
And of the Cannibals that each other eat,
The Anthropophagi, and men whose heads
Do grow beneath their shoulders.

[I, iii, 128–45]

Pory, being a scholar, was able to assess the debt that Africans and, incidentally, Elizabethans owed to Leo. English mariners, along with those of Europe, charted the coastline, but it was left to Leo to give factual information on the interior and to fill it with people rather than monsters. Pory wrote of Leo:

Like as our prime and peerless English antiquary Master William Camden in his learned *Britannia* hath exactly described England, Scotland, Ireland, and the isles adjacent . . . so likewise . . . John Leo in the history ensuing hath so largely, particularly, and methodically deciphered the countries of Barbarie, Numidia, Libya, the land of Negroes, and the hither part of Egypt as (I take it) never any

AFRICA

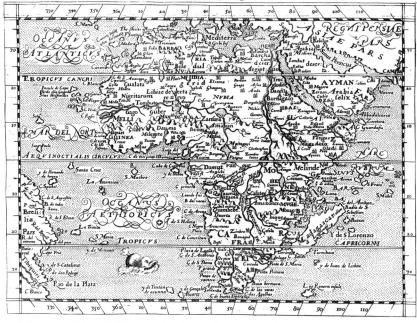

Illus. 10. Map of Africa in Pory's translation of Leo's *Geographical History.*

writer either before or since his time hath done. . . . So that the Africans may justly say to him, . . . "Wandering up and down like pilgrims in our own native soil, thy books have as it were led us the right way home; that we might at length acknowledge both who and where we are. Thou hast revealed the antiquity of our nation, the order of times, the rites of our religion, our manner of government both in peace and war, yea thou hast described the situations of countries and places" [sigs. [A]3v–[A]4r].

The Elizabethans certainly appreciated Leo and referred to him with great deference. The revered Hakluyt, who in fact encouraged Pory to undertake the translation, wrote in a prefatory "approbation," "I do hold and affirm it [Leo's *History*] to be the very best, the most particular, and methodical, that ever was written, or at least that hath come to light, concerning the countries, peoples, and affairs of Africa." It is a sobering thought that the discriminating Elizabethan reader knew more through this one book about the interior of Africa than many reputable scholars since then until about a quarter of a century ago.

One of the more popular objections raised against the idea that Shakespeare intended his Othello to be black is that the playwright could only have known "black Moors" (Negroes) as slaves. This is entirely wrong. Leo's very influential book details many of the kingdoms in "the land of the Negroes." Among the kingdoms described is "the kingdom of Tombuto" (Timbuktu), and the picture that emerges of that kingdom is of a well-ordered, prosperous, civilized society in which learning flourished as well as trade:

Howbeit there is a most stately temple to be seen, the walls whereof are made of stone and lime; and a princely palace also built by a most excellent workman of Granada. Here are many shops of artificers, and merchants, and especially of such as weave linen and cotton cloth. And hither do the Barbarie merchants bring cloth of Europe. . . . Corn, cattle, milk, and butter this region yieldeth in great abundance, but salt is very scarce here; for it is brought hither by land from Tegaza, which is five hundred miles distant. When I myself was here, I saw one camel's load of salt sold for 80 ducats. The rich king of Tombuto hath many plates and scepters of gold, some whereof weigh

1300 pounds, and he keeps a magnificent and well-furnished court.
. . . Here are great store of doctors, judges, priests, and other learned
men, that are bountifully maintained at the king's cost and charges.
And hither are brought divers manuscripts or written books out of
Barbarie, which are sold for more money than any other merchandise
[sigs. 2B6r–2B6v].

To the curious modern reader who might be inclined to ask why
this advanced civilization did not survive, Leo incidentally sup-
plied the answer: "And their town is much in danger of fire; at
my second being there half the town almost was burnt in five
hours space."

Samuel Coleridge's question about Othello therefore answers
itself. If Coleridge (like many cultivated Elizabethan gentlemen-
scholars and, we presume, Shakespeare) had read his Leo, he
would never have asked in haughty rhetoric: "Can we imagine
him [Shakespeare] so utterly ignorant as to make a barbarous
negro plead royal birth—at a time, too, when negroes were not
known except as slaves?" On this particular point, the ignorance
was not Shakespeare's.

Authentic information about the interior of Africa was now
available, and authors could use it as they wished. Leo became part of the canon. Samuel Purchas summarized his material
in *Hakluytus Posthumus* (1625) as did others, and each author's
fancy dictated what he chose to present in his popular summary.
It is interesting to see how Peter Heylyn in his *Microcosmus*
(1621) selected only uncomplimentary matter from Leo's material on the African kingdoms, often wading through a great deal
of complimentary material to pick out one trivial negative sen-
tence. One convenient example will illustrate the point. Out of
the long section on Tombuto (Timbuktu) from which an extract
has been given above, Heylyn selected only two sentences and
ignored all other matter. His summary reads: "Tombutum, where
the king causeth such as have any commerce with the Jews to be
slain, and where the people spend their whole lives in dancing
and singing." He enlarged his summary in subsequent editions
(1625, etc.), adding material on the king's wealth and style and
the entertainment of learned men in his court. Authentic informa-

tion was there, but successive generations of scholars chose to ignore it, or were completely unaware of its existence, until gradually new superstitions replaced the old and Africa once again became for Englishmen the dark continent. It was not quite so dark to Shakespeare and his contemporaries.

Tourists and Venturers

Although the activities of the Barbary pirates made voyages to North Africa hazardous, English merchant ships continued their trade with North Africa and even carried adventurous tourists as passengers. A reference has already been made to Windham's voyage to North Africa in 1551. Hakluyt's pages contain several accounts of the leisurely visits of Englishmen to North Africa and Egypt, places that became increasingly popular extensions of the grand tour during the second half of the century.

John Evesham started a tour on December 5, 1586, and visited Algiers, Tunis, Alexandria, Carthage, and Cairo. His account, published by Hakluyt, gives among other things a description of Alexandria with its underground waterworks built to control the annual inundation of the Nile. Hakluyt also recorded the journey of Laurence Aldersey to Alexandria and Cairo in 1586, as well as an anonymous "Pilgrimage to Mecca," the latter describing not only Alexandria and Cairo but also the Nile with its notorious crocodiles, which made journeys even along the banks hazardous. Accounts like these made the names of North African towns, phenomena like the inundation of the Nile and the elaborate device for measuring its rise and fall, and the animals of the Nile common enough currency for the dramatists to be able to make free use of them in their plays. When Shakespeare's Antony regales, albeit facetiously, the inebriated Lepidus with descriptions of the crocodile and the Nile, he is doing no more than any Elizabethan Englishman would have been expected to do, in exchange for his supper, on his return from faraway places.

In addition to accounts of private journeys, Hakluyt's pages abound with accounts of trading voyages to North Africa and

Illus. 11. A drawing of a crocodile of the Nile from Pierre Belon's *La nature et diversité des poissons* (Paris, 1555).

the perils risked by sailors from pirates, capricious Moorish potentates, renegades, and traitors, not to mention the natural hazards of wind and storm. Hakluyt, whose shorter work had appeared in 1589, provided the dramatists with all the background they needed for their plays set in Africa. It is against such a background that Shylock muses on the risks involved in such a trading voyage—he had an argosy going to Tripolis among other places— "But ships are but boards, sailors but men: there be land rats and water rats, land thieves, and water thieves—I mean pirates—and then there is the peril of waters, winds, and rocks" (*Merchant of Venice*, I, iii, 22–26). Antonio fears at one time that his ships "have all miscarried," but they turn up quite unexpectedly later:

> three of your argosies
> Are richly come to harbor suddenly.
>
> [V, i, 276–77]

Hakluyt's pages made both the risks involved in the trade and the sudden changes of fortune quite credible to Elizabethan audiences.

One example of an account with all the ingredients of a melo-drama will suffice to illustrate the sort of narration that would have fired the imagination of a playwright like Thomas Heywood, while preparing an audience for his rambling plots. Hakluyt reproduced in full the account of "The voyage made to Tripolis in Barbarie, in the year 1583 with a ship called the Jesus, wherein the adventures and distresses of some Englishmen are truly reported, and other necessary circumstances observed." The narrative fully lives up to the promise of its lengthy title. Before the expedition had even cleared the coast of England, its participants had lost two captains by death. They arrived in Barbary after sundry storms, only to be cheated by the king of Tripolis to their heavy loss. When they set sail, they were recalled by a heavy barrage of gunfire because one of their number had smuggled a debtor on board. They were thrown in prison and later arraigned and sentenced, two of them to death. At the intervention of an English factor, the king pardoned the captain, only to change his mind immediately afterward. Thomas Sanders, the narrator, at this stage commented:

Here all true Christians may see what trust a Christian man may put in an infidel's promise, who being a king, pardoned a man now, . . . and within an hour after hanged him for the same cause before a whole multitude: and also promised our factors their oils custom free, and at their going away made them pay the uttermost penny for the custom thereof [II, Q4r].

One of the condemned men offered to "turn Turk" to save his life but was executed even after he had changed his faith. The others, including the author, were sentenced to perpetual slavery. Sanders was put on short rations and subjected to various forms of forced labor including a spell in the galleys. In spite of all this, Sanders, like Antonio's ships, richly came to harbor. By a chain of influence, his father got Queen Elizabeth to intervene with the Great Turk himself, who ordered the release of the survivors and a full restitution of all their losses.

Elizabethan plays are full of the risks of North African trade — the treachery of Moorish kings, piracy, slavery, renegation, sud-

Illus. 12. Portrait of a Moorish nobleman sent on an embassy by the king of Morocco to Queen Elizabeth in 1600. From the portrait in the possession of the Shakespeare Institute, Birmingham, England, and here reproduced by permission of the Director.

den turns of fortune—for which published accounts of actual voyages made contemporary audiences receptive. The implausibilities in Heywood's rambling play *The Fair Maid of the West* seem quite credible beside the actual adventures of Sanders.

Elizabeth and the Moors

As the above account implies, Queen Elizabeth sometimes intervened. She had contacts, sometimes official consulates, in various Mediterranean ports. A portrait now in the possession of the Shakespeare Institute of Birmingham has for its subject a Moorish nobleman sent by the king of Morocco on an embassy to Queen Elizabeth in 1600. Pory referred to this ambassador in the letter dedicating his translation of Leo's *History* to Sir Robert Cecil when he wrote: "And at this time especially I thought they would prove the more acceptable in that the Moroccan ambassador . . . hath so lately treated with your Honor concerning matters of that estate."

Among the Queen's transactions with North African rulers was one that earned her the wrath of Rome. She had made a secret treaty with Abd-el-Malek by which she sent him cannon balls in exchange for saltpeter. These, according to irate Catholics, were the very cannon balls with which the forces of the Catholic king, Sebastian of Portugal, had been routed at the Battle of Alcázar in 1578. Elizabeth's reception of Abd-el-Malek's ambassador had been so warm that it aroused the jealousy of the Portuguese ambassador, who lodged a protest against it in London. The Queen was widely regarded by Catholics as being responsible for the defeat and death of Sebastian. In the words of the papal nuncio in Spain: "There is no evil that is not devised by that woman, who, it is perfectly plain, succoured Molucco [Abd-el-Malek] with arms, and especially with artillery."

The Battle of Alcázar also involved a legendary Englishman, Captain Thomas Stukely, and thus generated a great deal of interest in Africa among Englishmen. It led directly to George Peele's play, *The Battle of Alcazar*, which contained the first full-

THE
HISTORIE OF
THE VNITING
OF THE KINGDOM OF
PORTVGALL TO THE
Crowne of Caſtill:

*Containing the laſt warres of the Portugals againſt
the Moores of Africke, the end of the houſe
of Portugall, and change of that
Gouernment.*

The deſcription of Portugall, their principall Townes, Caſtles,
Places, Riuers, Bridges, Paſſages, Forces, Weakeneſſes, Reuenues,
and Expences. Of the Eaſt Indies, the Iſles of Terceres,
and other dependences, with many battailes by
ſea and lande, skirmiſhes, encounters,
ſieges, orations, and ſtratagemes
of warre.

*Imprinted at London by Arn. Hatfield
for Edward Blount.*

1600.

Illus. 13. Title page of Girolamo Franchi di Conestaggio's *The History of the Uniting of . . . Portugal to the Crown of Castile* (London, 1600), one of the many publications containing accounts of the Battle of Alcázar which was the subject of George Peele's play of the same name.

length portrait of a Negro character on the English stage. Peele was following a popularly accepted notion in making his hero, Muly Hamet, black, since it was well known that Muly was the son of a Negro mother. One account of the battle reads:

Now the cruel King Mulla Abdulla, amongst many other, taking to his wife a bondwoman, that was a black Negro, had by her a son called Mulla Sheriffa [Muly of Peele's play] who for that he was of his mother's complexion was commonly called the Black King [H. de Castries, *Le sources inédites d'Angleterre de l'histoire du Maroc* (1918–35), I, 332].

The Poetic Image

The image of Africa that emerges from the sixteenth-century Englishmen's knowledge of Africa is a composite one—Othello, for example, seems to be a blend of characteristics popularly attributed to North African Moors with the color known to be more common in West Africa, and called no more erroneously then than now, black. Elizabethans knew Africans as free men; they also knew them as slaves. They traded with them, they fought with them, they captured them, they killed them. They learned new facts about them, but they never really forgot the old tales of Pliny and Herodotus. Africans were at the same time well known and yet strange; thus there was plenty of room for the imagination to make what it would of them.

In as late a play as *Othello*, the image of the Anthropophagi could be invoked, even though no eyewitness accounts had described an encounter with one of them. *Selimus* too refers to men

> More bloody than the Anthropophagi,
> That fill their hungry stomachs with man's flesh.
>
> [III, vi, 77–78]

A more complete catalogue occurs in *Locrine:*

> If the brave nation of the Troglodites,
> If all the coal-black Aethiopians,
> If all the forces of the Amazons,
> If all the hosts of the barbarian lands,

Illus. 14. Map of Africa from Ortelius's *Theatrum orbis terrarum.*

Should dare to enter this our little world,
Soon should they rue their over-bold attempts.

[IV, i]

For *Tamburlaine the Great, Part II,* Christopher Marlowe used
the then fairly recent map that Abraham Ortelius first published
in his *Theatrum orbis terrarum* in 1570. As Ethel Seaton has
shown (*Essays and Studies,* X [1924], 13–35), Marlowe must
have had this map open in front of him when he wrote Techelles's
speech in which he describes his great march over Africa, for the
details follow the map very closely. The name Zanzibar, it will be
noted, is located on the western part of Africa as in the map.
Zanzibar disappears from this part of Africa in later maps and
becomes confined to the island on the east coast which is now part
of Tanzania. (See for example, the ornamented map of Africa of
1631 appended to this booklet.) Marlowe's lines, following the
earlier map, read:

And I have marched along the river Nile,
To Machda, where the mighty Christian priest
Called John the Great, sits in a milk-white robe,
Whose triple miter I did take by force,
And made him swear obedience to my crown.
From thence unto Cazates did I march
Where Amazonians met me in the field:
With whom (being women) I vouchsafed a league,
And with my power did march to Zanzibar
The western part of Afric, where I viewed
The Ethiopian sea, rivers, and lakes:
But neither man nor child in all the land.
Therefore I took my course to Manico,
Where unresisted I removed my camp;
And by the coast of Byather at last
I came to Cubar where the Negroes dwell.
And conquering that, made haste to Nubia,
There having sacked Borno the kingly seat,
I took the king, and led him bound in chains
Unto Damasco, where I stayed before.

[I, vi, 59–78]

MORO DE BARBARIA

Illus. 15. Drawing of a Moor in Cesare Vecellio's *Degli habiti antichi et moderni* (Venice, 1590).

Africa was for the Elizabethans always a land of strange monsters, particularly serpents and crocodiles, the latter bred out of the Egyptian slime. The crocodile's proverbial imperviousness to missiles is reflected in Marlowe's lines in *Tamburlaine:*

> As crocodiles that unaffrighted rest
> While thundring cannons rattle on their skins.
>
> [*Part I*, IV, i, 10–11]

African Stage Characters

For most Englishmen, Africans were predominantly thought of as black. They had better evidence; many accounts, beginning with Eden's, had indicated that Africans were of different colors, but black was a more dramatic contrast with the European complexion—it was also conveniently symbolic. Thus most of the African characters portrayed on the English stage were black—Muly Hamet, Aaron, Eleazer, Othello, and the several Zanches or Zanthias were all black.

But there were white Moors too on the English stage. The Prince of Morocco in *The Merchant of Venice* is described in the first folio edition as a "tawny Moor" (an Elizabethan variant of "white Moor"), as is Abdelmelec (in contrast to Muly Hamet) in *The Battle of Alcazar*. Shakespeare even (alone among her portrayers) gave Cleopatra a touch of color and made her describe herself as I "that am with Phoebus's amorous pinches black." Philo also refers contemptuously to her "tawny front," thus indicating a sun-tanned complexion.

Stage characters with black faces, purporting to come from Africa and surrounding areas, even preceded the actual visits to Africa by Englishmen. Indeed the practice of blackening the faces of characters like the king of Egypt goes back to the English medieval mummers play. In the courtly "disguisings" of the sixteenth century, Africans were frequently portrayed by the masquers. In one such "disguising" in 1510, Henry VIII and the Earl of Essex appeared "appareled after Turkey fashion." His torch-

Illus. 16. Another Moor from Vecellio's *Degli habiti.*

bearers, however, were "appareled in crimson satin and green, like Moreskoes [Moors], their faces black." At least two of six ladies in the same show appeared as Egyptians, "their heads rolled in pleasance and tippers like the Egipcians, embroidered with gold. Their faces, necks, arms, and hands covered with fine pleasance black . . . so that the same ladies seemed to be nigrost [*sic*] or black Moors" (Edward Hall, *Henry VIII*, ed. C. Whibley [London, 1904] I, 15–17).

"Moors" were also used in the outdoor processions of the six-teenth century; one such character appeared in a pageant given by the London Drapers in 1522. A list of the expenses for that pageant includes "payment of 5s. to John Wakelyn, for playing the king of the Moors, (the company finding him his apparel, his stage, and his wildfire)." The wildfire (fireworks) was meant to clear a way through the crowds for the main procession. In George Peele's pageant, given on the occasion of the installation of Sir Wolstan Dixie as Lord Mayor of London in 1585, the pre-senter of the pageant is described as "him that rode . . . before the pageant, appareled like a Moor." No doubt his function at the head of the pageant was similar to Wakelyn's.

The accounts of the Office of Revels refer to expenses con-nected with the production of several masques of Moors during the reigns of Edward VI, Elizabeth, and James I. Some of these references show that in representing black Moors, the adjective "black" was literally interpreted. A masque of young Moors in which King Edward took part (at Shrovetide, 1548) illustrates the thoroughgoing attempts made to make these characters ap-pear black. They wore face masks and elbow-length gloves of black velvet and leggings of black leather. Among the expenses were: "To Richard Lees of London, mercer, for eight yards [and a] half of black velvet for gloves above the elbow for Moors . . . . To Hugh Eston the King's hosier for the making of fourteen pairs of nether stocks of leather black for Moors . . . . To Nicholas Modena, stranger . . . for the trimming, coloring, and lining of sixteen vizzards or masks for Moors" (Folger MS L.b. 6).

Queen Anne seems to have been particularly anxious to appear

Illus. 17. Inigo Jones's design for the costume of one of the Negro nymphs in Ben Jonson's *Masque of Blackness* (1605). Drawing in the Devonshire Collection, Chatsworth, England. Reproduced by permission of the Trustees of the Chatsworth Settlement.

as a Negro woman in a masque, and in deference to her wish, Ben Jonson made his principal characters in *The Masque of Blackness* "twelve nymphs, Negroes, and the daughters of Niger." Jonson and Inigo Jones collaborated to produce a very elaborate show with carefully designed scenery and costumes. Jones's design for the costume of one of these nymphs still survives and is in the Devonshire collection at Chatsworth. This and Henry Peacham's drawing of a scene from *Titus Andronicus,* showing Aaron, are the only two pictorial representations we have today of black characters as they appeared in the theatrical productions of the period. Both drawings show the characters as black. It seems clear from the evidence available that Peele's Muly Hamet in *The Battle of Alcazar,* Eleazer in *Lust's Dominion,* Othello, Zanche in John Webster's *The White Devil,* and a number of Zanches or Zanthias in other plays were all portrayed, like Aaron in the contemporary drawing, as black.

While on the subject of contemporary drawings of Moors it is as well to mention the popular emblem books in which proverbial sayings, notions, and mottoes were illustrated by accompanying drawings. To illustrate the idea of impossibility, Andrea Alciati, the Italian emblematist (1492–1550), had shown a picture of two white men trying to change the color of a Negro by scrubbing him. The accompanying lines were:

> Abluis Aethiopem; quid frustra?
> Ah desine. Noctis illustrare nigrae nemo potest tenebras.
>
> [You wash an Ethiopian; why the vain labor?
> Desist. No one can lighten the darkness of black night.]

Alciati's emblem books were very popular all over Europe throughout the century, and were frequently imitated. The English emblematist, Geoffrey Whitney, used the same basic motif for his *Choice of Emblems* in 1586, and he provided an even more elaborate accompanying verse in English:

> Leave off with pain, the blackamoor to scour,
> With washing oft, and wiping more than due
> For thou shalt find, that Nature is of power,

45

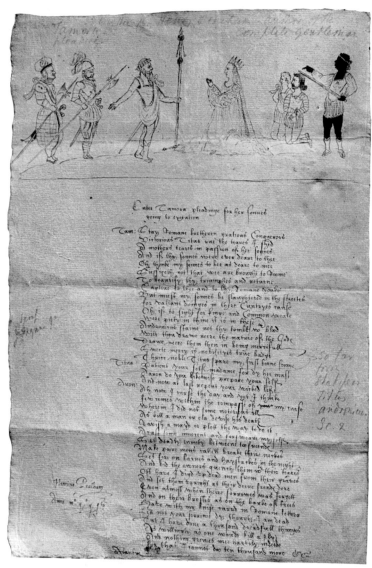

Illus. 18. A unique drawing by a contemporary, Henry Peacham, of a sixteenth-century production of a scene in Shakespeare's *Titus Andronicus*. From the collection at Longleat House, England. Reproduced by permission of the Marquess of Bath.

L EAVE of with paine, the blackamore to ſkowre,
With waſhinge ofte, and wipinge more then due:
For thou ſhalt finde, that Nature is of powre,
Doe what thou canſte, to keepe his former hue:
Thoughe with a forke, wee Nature thruſte awaie,
Shee turnes againe, if wee withdrawe our hande:
And thoughe, wee ofte to conquer her aſſaie,
Yet all in vaine, ſhee turnes if ſtill wee ſtande:
    Then euermore, in what thou doeſt aſſaie,
    Let reaſon rule, and doe the thinges thou maie.

Erafmus ex Luciano.
*Abluis Æthiopem fru-
ſtra: quin deſinis arte?
Haud vnquā efficies
nox ſit vt atra, dies.*
Horat. 1. Epiſt. 10.
*Naturam expellas fur-
ca tamen vſque re-
ſurret.*

——— *equuſq́;*
Nunquam ex degeneri fiet generoſus aſello,
Et nunquam ex ſtolido cordatus fiet ab arte.

Anulus in pict.
poëſi.

                                   H   *Non*

Illus. 19. Emblem illustrating "Impossible" from Geoffrey Whitney's *A Choice of Emblems* (Leiden, 1586).

Do what thou canst, to keep his former hue.
Though with a fork, we Nature thrust away,
She turns again if we withdraw our hand.
And though we oft to conquer her assay,
Yet all in vain, she turns if still we stand:
Then evermore, in what thou doest assay,
Let reason rule and do the things thou may.

[Sig. H1r]

The proverb in various forms—"You wash an Ethiop" or "You labor in vain (to wash an Ethiop white)" and other variants of it—are found dozens of times in Elizabethan and Jacobean writings. It was so popular that it was seldom quoted in full. Everyone in the audience of John Fletcher's play *The Knight of Malta* would have seen the allusion immediately when Oriana's black maid Zanthia was referred to as "My little labor in vain."

The stage stereotype of the black Moor was Muly Hamet, from whom a whole line of black Moors descended. These figures were usually embodiments of villainy, needing no elaborate psychological reason for their character; they were bad because they were black. In the symbolism of the age, they were equated with devils. Muly Hamet and his two black henchmen are thus described in *The Battle of Alcazar:*

> this tyrant king,
> Of whom we treat, sprung from the Arabian moor
> Black in his look and bloody in his deeds,
>
> . . .
>
> Accompanied as now you may behold,
> With devils coted in the shapes of men.

[ll. 17–23]

Aaron too reveled in his villainy:

> Let fools do good and fair men call for grace,
> Aaron will have his soul black like his face.

[*Titus Andronicus*, III, i, 205–6]

Shakespeare did make some attempt to give Aaron a vestige of humanity, but it was only later in *Othello* that even he really concerned himself with the psychology of a black character. Eleazer in *Lust's Dominion* is a black Machiavellian whose whole life is dominated by revenge. He too elicits the comparison with the devil because of his color as he bitterly says:

> The Queen with me, with me, a Moor, a Devil,
> A slave of Barbary, a dog, for so
> Your silken courtiers christen me.
> [*Lust's Dominion*, ll. 227–29]

A token reason for his unrelenting villainy is given to Eleazer, but this is not very seriously treated in the play. The playwright felt little need for psychological niceties. The man's color was enough explanation for his behavior. Eleazer is also lustful (as is Aaron), a trait commonly attributed to dark-skinned peoples.

It was Shakespeare in *Othello* who for the first time presented a Negro as a reasonable human being with credible psychology to which his blackness made a significant contribution, but only a contribution. Shakespeare thus effected a humanization of what was for his contemporaries essentially a type character. Curiously, Shakespeare's portrayal seems to have exhausted dramatic interest in the male Moor; there was no other significant treatment after Othello until the Restoration.

African characters were popular for a time on the Elizabethan and Jacobean stages, but the use of that continent as a source of images was even more pervasive; too much so to be detailed here. (A glance at E. H. Sugden's *Topographical Dictionary* [Manchester, London, New York, 1925] under headwords like Africa, Barbary, Guinea, Ethiopia, Moor, Blackmoor, and Negro would quickly reveal the extent.) There were thousands of references in the prose and the poetry of the period to the continent, its peoples, and its products. Its reputed wealth in gold made it the summation of earthly bliss for Ancient Pistol, who announced the coronation of Prince Hal with the words: "I speak of Africa and golden joys" (2 *Henry IV*, V, iii, 104). Its reputation for producing strange beasts and monsters provided the background for Aufidius's expression of hatred for Coriolanus:

> Not Afric owns a serpent I abhor
> More than thy fame.
>
> [*Coriolanus*, I, viii, 3–4]

The individual areas were even more frequently used than the continent as a whole. Barbary horses, Barbary hens, Barbary pigeons, and the gold of Barbary became as common currency as Guineas, Guinea hens, Guinea pigmies, and even Guinea toothpicks! Allusions to Egypt, its Nile, its crocodiles, and its other serpents bred of Nilus's slime were also numerous—the frequent treatment of Cleopatra alone made this almost inevitable. Egypt's fame as a seat of magic is glanced at in the history of Othello's handkerchief. Juliet appeared against the background of night "like a rich jewel in an Ethiop's ear" (*Romeo and Juliet*, I, v, 48), while, because of her coloring, Julia in *Two Gentlemen of Verona* drew an unfavorable comparison with a "swarthy Ethiope" (II, vi, 26).

To conclude, geographers, merchants, seamen, and scholars all participated in the great interest that Africa aroused in the sixteenth and seventeenth centuries. The poets and playwrights gratefully accepted their opportunity and spiced their plays with characters and references from this exciting and, for them, new continent. For most of them Africa was only a new vogue to be transiently exploited as a means of enhancing the poetry and the spectacle of their plays. Out of this passing fashion, Shakespeare uniquely created something abiding in *Othello*.

Suggested Reading

EARLY PRINTED BOOKS

Boemus, Johann, *The Fardle of Fashions,* tr. William Waterman. London, 1555; repr. Edinburgh, 1888.
Eden, Richard, *The Decades of the New World . . . Written in . . . Latin . . . by Peter Martyr of Angleria.* London, 1555.
——, *The History of Travel,* ed. Richard Willes. London, 1577.
Hakluyt, Richard, *The Principal Navigations.* London, 1598–1600; repr. Glasgow, 1903–5.
Leo Africanus, Joannes, *A Geographical History of Africa,* tr. John Pory. London, 1600; repr. as *History and Description of Africa,* ed. Robert Brown, London, 1896.
Mandeville, Sir John, *The Voyages and Travels.* London, 1583?

GENERAL WORKS

Blake, John W., *Europeans in West Africa, 1450–1560.* London, 1942.
Bovill, Edward W., *The Battle of Alcazar.* London, 1952.
——, *The Golden Trade of the Moors.* London, 1958.
Cawley, Robert R., *The Voyagers and Elizabethan Drama.* London, 1938.
Chew, Samuel C., *The Crescent and the Rose.* New York, 1937.
Jones, Eldred D., *Othello's Countrymen.* London, 1965.
Steele, Mary S., *Plays and Masques at Court.* New Haven, London, 1926.
Withington, Robert, *English Pageantry.* Cambridge, Mass., 1918–20.
Wright, Louis B., *Middle-Class Culture in Elizabethan England.* Chapel Hill, N.C., 1935; repr. Ithaca, N.Y., 1958, 1963.

SOME ELIZABETHAN AND JACOBEAN PLAYS WITH AN AFRICAN INTEREST
(The date each play was written is given in parentheses.)

Fletcher, John, *The Knight of Malta* (1616).
Heywood, Thomas, *The Fair Maid of the West* (1600/1603).
Jonson, Ben, *The Masque of Blackness* (1605).
Lust's Dominion (1599); conjecturally identified with *The Spanish Moor's Tragedy* by Dekker, Haughton, and Day.
Marston, John, *The Wonder of Women; or, The Tragedy of Sophonisba* (1606).
Peele, George, *The Battle of Alcazar* (1589).
Shakespeare, William, *Antony and Cleopatra* (1606).
——, *The Merchant of Venice* (1596).
——, *Othello* (1604).
——, *Titus Andronicus* (1589 or 1590).